THE *POWER* OF

Blessing

YOUR

Children

THE *POWER* OF *Blessing* *YOUR* *Children*

MARY RUTH SWOPE

WHITAKER
HOUSE

The Power of Blessing Your Children

ISBN: 978-1-60374-125-5
eBook ISBN:978-1-60374-455-3
Printed in the United States of America
© 1992, 2010 by Mary Ruth Swope

Swope Enterprises, LLC
7357 FM 161 South
Avinger, Texas 75630
www.maryruthswope.com

Whitaker House
1030 Hunt Valley Circle
New Kensington, PA 15068
www.whitakerhouse.com

9 10 11 12 13 14 15 **UU** 25 24 23 22 21 20

Dedication

This book is dedicated first of all to my grandson, Joseph Daniel Darbro.

Second, I dedicate this book to all parents and grandparents in the whole world who want to have a godly influence on their children and grandchildren, even when their residences are not in close proximity to their family members.

Acknowledgments

The idea for this little book was an inspired one. It came together so smoothly and quickly as to be unreal, judging from my previous experience in writing and publishing. Those dear friends who made contributions include:

+ my granddaughter, Elise Michelle Darbro;
+ my partner, Charlotte Bates;
+ my proofreader, Peter Chambers;
+ my friends, Dick and Christine Deitsch;
+ my assistant, Kandi Nolen;
+ my editor, Val Cindric; and
+ my daughter, Susan Cornwell Darbro.

As I always like to say, for strength, health, life, and years of education and experience—all needed for a task of this nature—I give thanks to God.

Contents

Part Three: The Fruit of Blessing

Part One:

The Concept of Blessing

How It Started with Me

During my prayer time one morning, I was musing over the fact that I lived so far away from my daughter's only child, Joseph Daniel Darbro. It saddened me to think that I would not have the opportunity to influence his spiritual, social, emotional, and physical development in the same way that my maternal grandmother had influenced mine.

From the time my Grandmother Lutz came to live in our home when I was six months old, she was the one who read me stories, said prayers with me, helped me memorize poetry, and played games with me. I fondly remember the happy hours we spent together as she taught me to sew, knit, crochet, tat, and quilt.

My grandmother became the ideal role model for me, and I learned from watching her what it means to be a Christian servant and community leader. Not only did she regularly teach Sunday school and take an active part in church women's groups, she also served on the boards of several community organizations.

As I thought about her life and the tremendous impact she had made on mine, I longed to do the same for my precious seven-year-old grandson Daniel. But I knew the many miles separating us made it impossible for me to be with him regularly.

Then, one day, I remembered the testimony of a Baptist pastor who had suddenly been dismissed from his post. Shocked over the dismissal and brokenhearted by the aftermath of events, the pastor was depressed and lonely. To make matters worse, many of the other clergymen in his area shunned him, leaving him feeling devastated.

A few days later, however, one of his good friends—the local Jewish rabbi—came to express his sadness over the unfortunate affair. "I want to do more than extend my condolences," the rabbi said. "I've come to bless you." Those words took on deep spiritual meaning as the rabbi shared with the pastor the traditions of the Jewish faith regarding blessings.

"I believe that God's blessing on the Jewish people is a direct result of Jewish parents regularly blessing their children," the rabbi said. He noted that the majority of Nobel and Pulitzer prizes have been awarded to Jewish men and women, and that a large percentage of America's millionaires are Jewish people, even though they make up only 2.7 percent of the population.

As a result of the rabbi's visit, the pastor began to study the phenomenon of *blessing* in the Scriptures. Before long, he started teaching other fathers to bless their spouses and children on a daily basis, and this opened many new doors of ministry for him throughout the country.

The pastor's testimony and the rabbi's words were brought back to my mind as I wondered how I could have a positive influence on my grandson's life. I thought, *Why can't I begin to bless my grandson every time I speak to him on the telephone? That would be a way to transfer my personal and spiritual values to Daniel when I cannot be physically present with him.*

Immediately, I began to write blessings.

The next time I phoned Daniel, I told him I wanted to bless him. He listened intently and then responded sweetly, "Thank you, Grandmother."

Four days later, I gave him a second blessing. The third time I called, I was ready to say good-bye when he asked, "Grandmother, are you going to bless me today?"

My heart almost leaped out of my chest as I realized that God was confirming to me how meaningful the blessings had been to my precious grandson.

Now, on a regular basis, I bless Daniel over the phone, focusing on a different area of his body, his personality, or his spiritual, physical, and emotional needs. I now feel closer to him than ever before!

I want other parents and grandparents to receive the same joy I have experienced from using this scriptural method of speaking a short blessing aloud.

The purpose of this little book is to encourage parents and grandparents to bless their children and grandchildren in the holy name of Jehovah God. It is He who forgives all sin. It is He who heals our bodies, souls, and spirits. He is the One who ransoms us from hell and who surrounds us with tender mercies and loving-kindness.

We can expect God to do great and marvelous deeds when we call forth the promises of His Word for our loved ones. As you bless your children in the name of the Lord, you will see God fill their lives with good things and bring full salvation even to your children's children. (See Psalm 103:17–18.)

The Beginning of God's Blessings

Once I discovered the wonderful experience of blessing my grandchild, I decided to research the origin of blessings to make sure that what I was doing was scriptural. I opened my Bible, and it soon became clear that the sovereign God of the universe had initiated the concept of blessing. It was His idea and not man's.

Within the first thirty-four verses of the Bible, I found that the word *blessing* is used three times.

In Genesis 1:22, God blessed the great sea creatures, all the creatures that live in the water, and the winged birds when He said, *"Be fruitful and multiply, and fill the waters in the seas, and let birds multiply on the earth."*

In Genesis 1:28, after God created the human male and female in His image, He blessed them by saying, *"Be fruitful and multiply; fill the earth and subdue it; have dominion over the fish of the sea, over the birds of the air, and over every living thing that moves on the earth."*

The third use of the word *bless* occurs in Genesis 2:3: *"Then God blessed the seventh day and sanctified it, because in it He rested from all His work which God had created and made."*

In these three instances, God's blessing consecrated what He blessed and set it apart for a special purpose. The things He blessed were:

- the creatures He created by His words (the fish and the birds);
- the creatures He created by His works (the male and the female);
- His—and our—day of rest (the seventh day of the week).

God had a reason for instituting the concept of blessing. It was necessary for the fulfillment of His purpose and plan for humanity here on earth. Knowing that Adam's fall would program the human race for death and not life, God instituted a covenant—a formal agreement of legal validity (a *blessing*)—to provide for man's success.

The Power of the Blessing

With each of God's blessings in Scripture, there was always a special anointing—an impartation of supernatural power that enabled the people He blessed. God's blessings:

- made impossible things possible;
- gave above-normal power, means, and ability for competency in living;

+ gave spiritual authority to our humanity.

Our forefather, Abraham, was the first man to receive the blessings of a covenant with God. This covenant contained seven promises, which are found in Genesis 12:2–3:

+ I will make you a great nation;
+ I will bless you;
+ I will make your name great;
+ you shall be a blessing;
+ I will bless those who bless you;
+ I will curse him who curses you;
+ and in you all the families of the earth shall be blessed.

Is that power for living or not? Yes, it is truly power enough to help us live successful lives for God. No wonder the enemy of our souls doesn't want us to bless our children!

We cannot allow Satan to rob us of this wonderful privilege. As believers and the heirs of God's kingdom, we must learn to take our authority and claim the rich inheritance promised to our children and grandchildren.

Activating God's Promises of Blessing

How do we become the recipients of those same covenant promises made to Abraham? By activating the power of the blessing! We do that by speaking words of blessing based on God's Word.

Remember, the same promise that God gave to Abraham has also been made to us as Abraham's offspring: *"In your seed all the nations of the earth shall be blessed, because you have obeyed My voice"* (Genesis 22:18).

The Source of all blessings on earth is God the Father, and they can become ours through His Son, Jesus Christ. When we acknowledge Jesus as our Savior and Lord, we become God's children and Abraham's seed.

By becoming members of the family of God, we receive full rights to the blessing of our father, Abraham. And, like Abraham, we can pass on God's blessing to our children and grandchildren, just as our forefathers did.

Abraham's son, Isaac, blessed his sons, Jacob and Esau, in a very practical way, invoking upon them *"the dew of* heaven,…the fatness of the earth, and plenty of grain and wine" (Genesis 27:28).

When Jacob was about to die, he called together his twelve sons and pronounced prophetic words over them, according to each son's individual character. *"He blessed them, every one with the blessing appropriate to him"* (Genesis 49:28 NASB).

I believe that this is how we should bless our children and grandchildren: with blessings that are appropriate to them and specially designed to suit their individual ages, characters, personalities, and talents. We also want to make sure that our blessings are in line with God's promises and fit in with His plans and purposes for the people we are blessing.

Remember, the most important goal for our children and grandchildren should be that they bring glory to God in all they say and do. If we keep that in mind, then our blessings will not become selfish or worldly in nature.

Our heavenly Father has provided a marvelous inheritance for His children. He has given us all things that pertain to life and godliness: physical, spiritual, material, and personal. Nothing has been omitted to help us have everything we need for truly good lives. God even promises to share with us His own glory and goodness. (See 2 Peter 1:3–4.)

God wants us to enjoy His blessings, but we can do that only when we have an understanding of the many promises of which we are heirs through faith in Jesus Christ. In the Appendix, you will find a list of resources that detail many of the promises God has made to us, His children.

In addition to claiming the promises found in the Scriptures, I use the Hebrew names of God to remind me of God's great power and many provisions. Let me share these with you.

Blessing Promises[1]

+ Through Jehovah-Tsidkenu, I have been made righteous. *"For He made Him who knew no sin to be sin for us, that we might become the righteousness of God in Him"* (2 Corinthians 5:21).

+ Through Jehovah-M'kaddesh, I am sanctified, made holy, and set apart for His purposes. *"May the God of peace Himself sanctify you completely; and may your whole spirit, soul, and body be preserved blameless at the coming of our Lord Jesus Christ"* (1 Thessalonians 5:23).

+ Through Jehovah-Shalom, I am given peace. *"The peace of God, which surpasses all understanding, will guard your hearts and minds through Christ Jesus"* (Philippians 4:7).

+ Through Jehovah-Shammah, the presence of Christ is within me. *"Do you not know that you are the temple of God and that the Spirit of God dwells in you?"* (1 Corinthians 3:16).

---

[1] The names of God are taken from: Larry Lea, *Could You Not Tarry One Hour?* (Lake Mary, FL: Creation House, 1987), 189.

- Through Jehovah-Rapha, I am healed and experience divine health. *"Bless the LORD, O my soul, and forget not all His benefits: who forgives all your iniquities, who heals all your diseases"* (Psalm 103:2–3).

- Through Jehovah-Jireh, I will see the Lord's provision. *"This Book of the Law shall not depart from your mouth, but you shall meditate in it day and night, that you may observe to do according to all that is written in it. For then you will make your way prosperous, and then you will have good success"* (Joshua 1:8).

- Through Jehovah-Nissi, the Lord is my Banner; I will always win. *"Thanks be to God, who gives us the victory through our Lord Jesus Christ"* (1 Corinthians 15:57).

- Through Jehovah-Rohi, the Lord is my Shepherd, and I have safety and guidance. *"My sheep hear My voice, and I know them, and they follow Me. And I give them eternal life, and they shall never perish; neither shall anyone snatch them out of My hand"* (John 10:27–28).

- Through Jehovah-Sabboath, all my needs are met, and I have total victory. *"He who did not spare His own Son, but delivered Him up for us all, how shall He not with Him also freely give us all things?"* (Romans 8:32).

Through the names of Jehovah God, every provision has been made for us to be blessed in this life, to receive salvation, and to experience eternal life. Our needs are met 100 percent!

As we consider the wonderful blessings and promises God has made available to us, praise wells up within our hearts, and we cry out with the psalmist:

Power belongs to God! His majesty shines down on Israel; his strength is mighty in the heavens. What awe we feel, kneeling here before him in the sanctuary. The God of Israel gives strength and mighty power to his people. Blessed be God!   (Psalm 68:34–35 TLB)

Bless Your Children and Grandchildren

As we appropriate God's all-encompassing blessings and promises into our own lives and learn to claim them for ourselves, it becomes our responsibility to pass them on to our children and grandchildren.

If you are a parent or grandparent and a member of the family of God through faith in the blood of Jesus Christ, you have spiritual authority over your household. You have authority and power to speak blessings into the lives of your children and grandchildren.

Your words of blessing are energized by the power of God when you speak them.

When you speak what God wills you to speak, your children and grandchildren's lives will begin to change. Their lives will begin to conform to your words, so be careful how you bless them and always be positive. Remember, once the blessings have been spoken, they cannot be stopped or thwarted by man or by the powers of darkness. (See the story of Jacob and Esau in Genesis 27.)

Our Lord Jesus Christ provides the best example of how to bless our children. When several parents brought their children to Jesus for Him to lay hands on them,

> *He took them up in His arms, laid His hands on them, and blessed them.* (Mark 10:16)

The New Testament speaks about "the laying on of hands" when a special gift or anointing is being given to someone. (See, for example, Acts 8:18; 9:17; 1 Timothy 4:14; 5:22; 2 Timothy 1:6; Hebrews 6:2.) I believe that it is important, whenever possible, to touch your children with gentleness and tenderness as you impart your words of blessing.

To get you started, I have provided examples of the blessings I have been speaking to my grandson. Each blessing is based on promises from the Bible, and the Scripture references are given at the end. There are forty-nine blessings—one for every day for seven weeks.

I'm sure that as this becomes a habit for you, your blessings will become more personal and specific, and wonderful changes will begin to take place in the lives of your family members. It is my prayer that from now until Jesus comes back, we will be found among those parents and grandparents who daily bless their children and grandchildren.

Now, let me bless *you* before you begin.

A Blessing for Parents and Grandparents

May the Lord bless you and keep you. May the Lord make His face shine upon you, and may He be gracious to you. May the Lord turn His countenance upon you and give you peace.

You have been chosen to be God's own possession. He is God, the faithful One, who shows loving-kindness and keeps His covenant promises to a thousand generations of those who love Him and obey His commandments. The Lord will keep His covenant of love with you, for you are holy to the Lord your God.

Let all these blessings that you speak by faith in the name of the Lord Jesus Christ rest on the heads of your beloved children and grandchildren now and for the rest of their lives.

Numbers 6:24–26 · Deuteronomy 7:6–9

Part Two:

The Content of Blessing

Abilities

In the name of Jesus Christ:

I bless you with the power to see with accuracy your special, God-given abilities. May you become a competent worker in the field of endeavor for which God has ordained you.

See yourself as a person with many latent talents. The Holy Spirit stands ready to help you understand and develop your gifts, so be bold in asking for His help.

May the gifts and fruit of the Holy Spirit to help others be evident in your life. I bless you with the anointing of God to fulfill His special purposes for your life.

Matthew 25:14–30 · Romans 12:4–8
1 Corinthians 12:4–11

Abundance

In the name of Jesus Christ:

I bless you with the abundance of goods that God has ordained for you to possess and use. May you have enough substance to lend to many others without ever having to borrow for your own needs.

May the Lord make you abound in all the works of your hands, in the fruit of your body, in the increase of your investments of time and energy, and in the produce of your land. He will bless you with plenty.

Deuteronomy 15:6; 30:9 · Psalm 92:12

Angels

In the name of Jesus Christ:

I bless you with a host of active angels whom God made to guard and rescue all who reverence Him. He will send these ministering spirits to protect His children from danger and to defend them from their enemies.

Your angels in heaven have constant access to your heavenly Father, and He orders them to protect you wherever you go. Throughout your life, they will steady you with their hands to keep you from stumbling over the stones along your pathway.

Do not be afraid; unseen warriors walk beside you.

Psalm 34:7; 91:11–12 · Matthew 4:11; 18:10
Hebrews 1:7

Assurance

In the name of Jesus Christ:

I bless you with the assurance that God will search for you if you are lost and will bind you up if you are broken and will strengthen you if you are sick. Indeed, He will always be seeking you as one of His sheep, and He will deliver you to a safe place if you wander off the right pathway.

He will never leave you or forsake you; the Lord is your helper, so do not fear. May you, the beloved of the Lord, rest securely in Him who surrounds you with His loving care and preserves you from every harm.

You may be sure that God will do what He has promised.

Genesis 28:15 • Deuteronomy 33:12 • Ezekiel 34:16
John 14:18 • Hebrews 13:6

Authority

In the name of Jesus Christ:

I bless you with the revelation that God has given you authority over all the power of the enemy (Satan) and that nothing will by any means harm you. No weapon formed against you will prosper.

You have been made to have dominion over the works of God's hands, and all those things have been put in subjection under your feet.

Therefore, do not be afraid. You can be victorious over the enemy of your soul. It is God's will to deliver you.

Psalm 8:6–8 • Isaiah 54:17 • Hebrews 2:7–8

Children

In the name of Jesus Christ:

I bless you with God's blessing to Adam and Eve when He said to them, *"Be fruitful and multiply; fill the earth and subdue it"* (Genesis 1:28).

Children are a gift from the Lord, and they are like arrows in the hand of a warrior. They will defend you. Your children will be like olive plants around your table. Yes, you will live to see your children's children, and peace will be upon your household.

Your family will obtain the favor of the Lord. In the name of Christ, the Lord, I bless you with wise and obedient children.

Psalm 127:4–5; 128:3, 6 • Proverbs 23:24 • Isaiah 54:13

Clear Direction

In the name of Jesus Christ:

I bless your going out and your coming in today and every day. May you ponder the ways of your feet and not turn to the right or to the left from the path that God has planned for you.

May you have clear direction on the road you are to walk today. When you allow the Lord to direct your steps, He takes delight in each move you make.

May you understand the lessons God is trying to teach you from what He permits to happen in your life. If you stay on God's pathway, your life will be filled with joy and gladness.

Psalm 32:8; 37:23; 121:8; 143:8, 10
Proverbs 4:21–23, 26; 8:20

A Controlled Tongue

In the name of Jesus Christ:

I bless your tongue. You will be a person who will learn early in life to weigh your words and measure your thoughts before you pour them forth from your mouth.

Your tongue will speak positive words that affirm and bless those who hear you. Your tongue will always tell the truth in love and will talk to others about good things. Your tongue will constantly find ways to bring happiness to others.

Without fail, your tongue will be used to glorify God and edify your family and friends. It will praise your God all day long.

Proverbs 21:23 • Ecclesiastes 3:7
Ephesians 4:15 • James 3:4

Courage

In the name of Jesus Christ:

I bless you with courage to stand in the face of fear and to know that God is your refuge and strength. You do not need to be afraid or terrified, for the Lord your God goes before you; He will never leave you or forsake you.

Every place where you set your foot will be a place of victory for you. No one will be able to stand up against you all the days of your life.

Fear is the opposite of faith, and God has not given you a spirit of fear. He has blessed you with power and love and a sound mind. That is the essence of courage.

Deuteronomy 31:6 · Joshua 1:3, 5 · 2 Timothy 1:7

Creativity

In the name of Jesus Christ:

Within you dwells the spirit of creativity, for you are made in the image of the great Creator, the Maker of heaven and earth. He is the One who gives you ideas to design, build, and perform. Let Him fill your imagination with creative thoughts that, when brought to reality, will bring glory to Him and blessings to others.

May the beauty of the Lord our God be upon you to establish the work of your hands.

Genesis 1:26–27 · 2 Chronicles 2:12–14
Psalm 90:17; 146:5–6

Deliverance

In the name of Jesus Christ:

You will know deliverance from evil and from all those who rise up against you. The eternal God is your refuge, and underneath you are the everlasting arms of your heavenly Father. He will drive out your enemies before you. God Almighty is your shield and your glorious sword.

Your enemies will cower before you, and you will trample down the objects of their idolatry. Blessed be God Most High, who delivers your enemies into your hand.

Deuteronomy 33:27, 29 • Psalm 44:4–5

Eternal Life

In the name of Jesus Christ:

I bless you with God's promise of eternal life, which is in Christ Jesus our Lord. He who believes in the Son of God has the witness of this life in himself. May you be among those who have believed in the Lord Jesus Christ and who are saved.

Someday you will see God's face, and His name will be on your forehead. Your name will be written in the Lamb's Book of Life.

May your faith in the name of Jesus Christ, which is above every name that is named in heaven and on earth, be your heritage and your gift to the generations who follow you.

John 3:16 • Romans 6:23 • 1 John 5:11
Revelation 21:27; 22:4

Eyes to See

In the name of Jesus Christ:

I bless your eyes. I command them to see in detail the exquisite design of everything that God made for our pleasure. May your eyes look up at the sky and see the beauty of the clouds and marvel at the stars, God's windows to heaven.

With equal intensity, see the created things upon and beneath the earth; marvel at their colors, shapes, and sizes—their perfection in every detail. Allow God to reveal Himself to you as you stand in amazement at these beautiful treasures and magnificent works of art.

Be filled with adoration for your God as your eyes forever discover new things about His glorious creation.

Psalm 8:3; 19:1 • Ecclesiastes 3:11 • Isaiah 33:17
Matthew 13:16

Faith

In the name of Jesus Christ:

I bless you with a special gift of faith—faith to believe that with God *all* things are possible—so that you can be brought into the place of highest honor and privilege in the things of God. Your faith will enable you to be completely sure that God is able to do anything He has promised. Because of this, you will be accepted and approved through your faith and become a friend of God like Abraham, our true example of abiding faith.

Without faith, it is impossible to please God; and without constantly hearing the Word of God, it is impossible to have faith. Remember that God rewards those who exercise their faith, for by faith, we have peace with God through the Lord Jesus Christ.

Romans 4:16, 21; 5:1–2 · Habakkuk 2:4 · Hebrews 11:6

Favor

In the name of Jesus Christ:

May you abound with the favor of the Lord, and may your life be full of blessing. Keep God's commands, and you will find favor not only with God but also with people. They will respect you for your good judgment and common sense, and your reputation will be one of honor.

Let your actions be pleasing to the Lord, and He will make even your enemies be at peace with you. As you grow in stature, may your heart grow in wisdom; thus, you will find favor, as Jesus did, with God and man.

Psalm 5:12 · Proverbs 3:1–4 · Luke 2:52

The Fear of the Lord

In the name of Jesus Christ:

I bless you with a reverential fear of God and the ability to highly respect the Lord. You will be happy and find great delight in keeping God's commands.

You will not be afraid of people—either great or small—or of what they say or do against you. Circumstances will never shake you from your foundation as long as you fear the Lord and obey His Word.

I bless you with great skill in hating those things that God hates: a prideful spirit, a lying tongue, an unruly mouth, and evil thoughts. His banner will be displayed over you because you recognize that He is the God of truth and righteousness.

Deuteronomy 5:29 · Psalm 25:12–14; 60:4; 128:1
Proverbs 6:16–19

A Free Spirit

In the name of Jesus Christ:

I bless you with freedom from stress and worldly care. Depression, frustration, and nervous anxiety over your circumstances are cursed forever. You will be able to face the natural events of your life with peace of mind and an inner joy that will dispel all negative emotions.

You will glorify your God by keeping His commandment not to worry about anything. Instead, you will pray about everything, telling Him your needs and thanking Him for the answers. You are blessed with a free spirit that is unaffected by worry.

Matthew 6:25–34 · John 14:27
Philippians 4:6–7 · 1 Peter 5:7

Good Health

In the name of Jesus Christ:

I bless you with good health all the days of your life. May you enjoy a healthy life in both body and soul so that you can continue to serve the Lord with great vigor and enthusiasm.

As you follow God's dietary guidelines found in the Bible, may the Lord remove from you all sickness and make your body immune to deadly diseases. If you do get ill, may you learn to claim the promises for healing and remember that we are healed by His stripes.

Do not be conceited or convinced of your own wisdom; instead, rely on the Lord and turn your back on evil. If you do that, you will be given renewed health and vitality.

Exodus 23:25 · Deuteronomy 7:15 · Proverbs 3:7–8
Isaiah 53:5 · 3 John 2

A Good Husband

In the name of Jesus Christ:

I bless you with a loving husband who will cleave to you and consider you as one with his own flesh. May he love you as Christ loves the church, and may he be willing to lay down his life for you.

May God choose for you a man who will remain faithful to you and always see in you the beauty of the woman he married. May he honor you as the gentler partner in your marriage and never do anything that will cause you grief or harm.

May he always provide for you in a way that will permit you to fulfill your duties as a wife and mother.

Genesis 2:24 · Proverbs 5:18–19 · Ephesians 5:25
1 Timothy 5:8 · 1 Peter 3:7

A Good Wife

In the name of Jesus Christ:

I bless you with a good wife who will love the Lord and obey His Word. May you live joyfully with her all the days of your life.

Because you fear the Lord and walk in His ways, you will be blessed by God with a wife who will be like a fruitful vine by the side of your house. Her price to you will be above that of rubies. A truly good wife is worth more than precious gems.

May the wife God chooses for you show you honor and respect and submit to you willingly out of her love for the Lord.

Psalm 128:1, 3 • Proverbs 18:22; 31:10–13
Ecclesiastes 9:9 • Ephesians 5:22–24

Hands That Bless

In the name of Jesus Christ:

I bless your hands. They will be hands that do kind things for other people. They will learn to work, doing all kinds of labor as unto the Lord. Your hands will be a blessing to you and to others as long as you live. May you prosper in everything you put your hand to do, and may your labors never be in vain.

I bless your fingers today. Those fingers will learn to play a musical instrument—the piano, flute, trumpet, violin, or other instrument. They will bless the Lord and other people with beautiful music.

May the Lord bless all your skills and be pleased with the work of your hands.

Deuteronomy 28:8 · Psalm 33:1–4; 90:17; 128:2
1 Thessalonians 4:11–12

Happiness

In the name of Jesus Christ:

I bless you with happiness and peace of mind. These gifts from God come only to those who love, trust, and obey the Lord. God always blesses those who follow His directions and who stay on His path.

If you do what is right and have confidence that your actions are pleasing to the Lord, you will never have to worry about what other people say about you. Happiness will be your reward. Happy and peaceful are those whose God is Jehovah.

Psalm 128:1–2 · Proverbs 16:20; 29:18 · Romans 14:22

Holiness

In the name of Jesus Christ:

I bless you with the will to turn your eyes from looking at worthless things and the resolve not to follow foolish people. Instead, you will permit God to open your eyes and let you see the wonderful things you can expect from respecting and obeying His laws. You will learn that His ways are perfect and that true holiness comes only through the shed blood of Jesus Christ.

Keep your hands clean and your heart pure; then, you will receive the blessings that come from living a life pleasing to the Lord.

Psalm 24:3–5; 119:18, 36–37 · Luke 1:74–75
Romans 12:1–2 · 2 Corinthians 7:1

The Holy Spirit

In the name of Jesus Christ:

I bless you with a full measure of the Holy Spirit of God. He is the One whom God sent to teach you all things, bring all things to your remembrance, show you things to come, guide you into all truth, make you an able minister, testify to you of Jesus Christ, convict you of sin, help you with your problems, empower you to witness, release your inhibitions toward holiness, seal you until the day of redemption, strengthen your inner man, and give you eternal life.

Open your heart and receive the Holy Spirit into your life, and all these blessings will be yours.

John 14:26; 15:26; 16:7, 13 • Acts 1:8 • Romans 8:26
2 Corinthians 3:6, 17 • Ephesians 1:13–15; 3:16

Hope

In the name of Jesus Christ:

I bless you with the truth that your God is a God of hope. He wants you never to give up in any situation, for He is forever your strong refuge.

I bless you with encouragement from God. May the God of all hope give you a full measure of hope today in your work and in your play.

Remember that hope is a gift to you from the Holy Spirit. God will fill you with joy and peace when you believe that He works all things together for your good and for His glory.

Psalm 43:5; 78:7 · Romans 15:13–14; 8:28
Colossians 1:5 · Hebrews 6:11

Humility

❦❦❦

In the name of Jesus Christ:

I bless you with a spirit of humility, which will cause you to acknowledge that all you have and all you are is the result of God's grace in your life.

May every joyful, happy, successful experience be combined with a spirit of humility. You will never be conceited over your successes, because wisdom will tell you that they are not a result of your own effort or talent. You will know that they are a gift to you—a blessing from your heavenly Father.

You will be free from feelings of inferiority, for God is going to give you an indomitable spirit—not a haughty spirit, but one of meekness and humility.

Psalm 69:32; 131:1–2 • Proverbs 22:4
Matthew 23:12 • James 4:6, 10

Joy

❧❦❧

In the name of Jesus Christ:

I bless you with a spirit of joy, because the joy of the Lord is your strength. I want you to be strong in body, in soul, and in spirit.

Let your joy come from the beauty of God's creative handiwork. See the trees. Look up at the sky and get joy from the beauty of the white, billowy clouds set against the blue horizon. See with your spiritual eyes the dozens of different birds God has made for your enjoyment. Take note of the detail in God's flowers—the colors, shapes, sizes, and perfumes.

Keep your mind on the things God has created for your pleasure and let them fill you with joy.

Nehemiah 8:10 • Psalm 28:7 • Isaiah 44:23; 55:12

Listening Ears

In the name of Jesus Christ:

I command your ears to hear clearly today. You will hear and understand with spiritual ears the Word of God. Like the wise man who built his house upon the rock, may you hear the sayings of Jesus and follow them. May the seed of the Word fall on fertile ground in your heart so that you will not only hear and understand but also bear and bring forth fruit a hundred times over.

You will also hear and heed the words of your parents and other elders. Their words of wisdom will be precious to you. I bless the ears of your heart so they will hear the words of knowledge and wisdom that are spoken to you today by God's righteous ones on earth.

Proverbs 18:15 · Matthew 7:24–25; 13:16, 23
Romans 2:13 · James 1:19–25

Longevity

In the name of Jesus Christ:

I bless you with the understanding that if you keep the commandments of God with all your heart, life will go well with you. Your days and those of your children will be multiplied, and the years of your lives will be lengthened by the Lord.

Loving God and keeping His commandments will not only prolong your life, but also bring protection from your enemies and the promise that you will not come to your grave until you are of full age, as a shock of corn comes in its season.

Exodus 20:12 · Deuteronomy 4:40 · Job 5:26
Psalm 91:16 · Proverbs 3:1–2, 9:11

Love

In the name of Jesus Christ:

I bless you with the will to love God with all your heart and with the ability to do so all the days of your life.

I also bless you with a deep desire to love both your parents with true affection for as long as you live. Loving God first and your parents next will undoubtedly lead to your loving yourself and your neighbors as yourself. I bless you with this kind of love.

I bless you with the understanding to grasp how wide and long and high and deep is the love of Christ for you. I flood you with the knowledge of how precious you are to God, to your family, and to your friends.

Exodus 20:12 · Deuteronomy 6:5; 10:12 · John 3:16
John 15:10, 12 · Romans 8:38–39 · Ephesians 3:17–19

Mercy

❦

In the name of Jesus Christ:

I bless you with the knowledge that the Lord is plenteous in mercy to everyone who calls on Him. Know that the Lord is good to all, and His tender mercies are over all His works.

I bless you with the desire to be faithful in showing kindness and mercy to your family and friends. God has promised to show favor and give a reward to those whose acts of mercy are done in the name of Jesus Christ.

Genesis 39:21 · Psalm 18:25; 86:5, 15; 145:8
Proverbs 3:3 · Matthew 5:7; 10:42

The Mind of Christ

In the name of Jesus Christ:

I bless you with the mind of Christ for your thoughts today. You will have the ability to think clearly and to be fair in your judgments. You will use your mind to glorify God on the earth today. Your mind will praise God as you fill it with Scripture.

I bless you with a spirit of wisdom, of knowledge, and of understanding. You will be blessed by God today for the way you use your mind. Your teachers will praise you for having wisdom beyond your years.

Isaiah 11:2–3 · 1 Corinthians 2:13, 16
Philippians 2:5–8 · Colossians 3:2

Ministry

In the name of Jesus Christ:

I bless you with the fulfillment of God's ordained plans for your occupation and ministry. The Lord has anointed you for very special purposes in an area of work and service to Him. He has said that you should go and bring forth fruit.

So arise, shine, and let the light and glory of the Lord come upon you. Seek the Lord and ask Him to show you clearly how and when and where to prepare for the occupation and ministry that He planned for you before the foundation of the world.

Isaiah 60:1 · John 15:16 · Romans 10:14–15
Ephesians 4:11–12 · 2 Timothy 2:15 · 1 Peter 2:9

Miracles

❈━━◆◈◆◈◆━━❈

In the name of Jesus Christ:

I bless you with the faith to believe for miracles in your life: miracles of healing, miracles of achievement, miracles of salvation, miracles of the mind, and miracles of guidance.

Look up. Reach out. Embrace them all. Your God is a God of miracles—all things are possible with Him. He brings His people forth with joy and His chosen ones with gladness because of His mighty, miracle-working power. Have the faith of a little child to believe God for the miraculous in your life.

Jeremiah 32:17, 27 · Matthew 19:26 · Acts 2:22
Ephesians 3:20 · James 5:13–15

Obedience

In the name of Jesus Christ:

I bless you with a submissive spirit that will joyfully and willingly obey the commands of God. Be careful to obey God's laws, and do not turn from them to the right or to the left so that you may be successful wherever you go.

May the Word of God not depart from your mouth, but may you meditate on it day and night, being careful to do all that is written in it. You will make your way prosperous, and you will have good success.

Joshua 1:7–8 · Psalm 1:1–6; 25:10
Proverbs 6:20–23 · Isaiah 1:19

Peace

❖❖❖

In the name of Jesus Christ:

I bless you with peace—another gift from God that comes to those who walk in His statutes and remember to do His commandments. Your children, too, will be taught about the Lord, and great will be their peace.

You will not be afraid but instead will have perfect peace if you keep your mind on Him. Jesus Christ is your peace. And the peace of God will keep your heart and mind in health as long as you trust and serve your God.

Isaiah 26:3; 54:13 • Psalm 29:11; 119:165 • John 14:27
Ephesians 2:14 • Philippians 4:7

Pleasant Words

In the name of Jesus Christ:

I bless you with an understanding of how important it is in life to set a guard over your mouth and to keep watch over the words that come from your lips. You will not speak negative and hurtful words that cause pain and wound spirits.

May you learn quickly that a soft answer turns away wrath and that words thoughtfully spoken bring great rewards with them. You will learn to express pleasant words, profitable advice, and kind speech in all your conversations.

Psalm 141:3 · Proverbs 15:23, 26; 16:24; 25:11
Luke 6:45 · Ephesians 4:29 · James 1:19

A Pleasing Personality

In the name of Jesus Christ:

I bless you with a pleasing personality. May the Lord give you the ability to be quick-witted, spontaneous, fun-loving, and full of laughter. You will be warmhearted toward your parents, your teachers, your neighbors, and your friends.

May you get along easily with all kinds of people, loving them with the love you receive daily from your heavenly Father. I bless you with a spirit of unity, that you may glorify God.

Because of your sweet spirit, others will consider you to be a channel through which God is shedding His light upon the earth.

Psalm 18:24 · Proverbs 15:13; 16:7 · Matthew 5:16
Romans 14:19 · Colossians 3:12–15 · 1 Peter 3:8

Praise

In the name of Jesus Christ:

I bless you with the desire to thank and praise God for everything He has done, is doing, and will do for you in your life.

I bless you with the ability to praise God with your voice in song, with your mouth in words, with your hands and feet in good deeds—and always from your heart.

Both riches and honor will be your reward, for God is merciful, gracious, long-suffering, and abounding in goodness to those whose hearts are full of praise.

Exodus 34:6–7 · Psalm 33:1–3; 96:1–4; 98:4–6
Ephesians 5:19 · Hebrews 13:15

Promotion

In the name of Jesus Christ:

I bless you with understanding, so that when you humble yourself, you will be exalted by your heavenly Father. When you are meek and lowly, God will bless you with the inheritance of the land.

You will know that all you have—and all you are—is because of what Jesus has done in and through your life.

You have been promoted to sit with Him in the heavenly realms. He has increased your greatness and given you comfort on every side by your promotion.

Psalm 76:6–7; 147:6 • Proverbs 22:4; 25:6–7
Matthew 5:5; 20:26; 23:12 • Ephesians 2:6

Prosperity

In the name of Jesus Christ:

I bless you with the prosperity with which God blessed the Israelites. He will look on you favorably and make you fruitful. He will multiply you and confirm His covenant with you.

God will give you rain in its season; your land will yield its produce, and the trees of your fields will yield their fruit. You will eat your bread to the full and dwell safely in your land. As long as you seek the Lord, He will prosper you.

Leviticus 26:3–5, 9 · 2 Chronicles 26:5
Psalm 1:3; 84:11 · 3 John 2

Protection

⊰❖⊱

In the name of Jesus Christ:

I bless you with the knowledge that in the time of trouble, your heavenly Father will hide you. He will set you on a high rock out of the reach of all your enemies. He will rescue you from every trap and protect you from the fatal plague.

Your God will shield you with His wings. His faithful promises will always be your armor. Don't be afraid, for God is with you.

I bless you with protection from all the powers of the enemy. In dangerous and distressing situations, may the God of Jacob send His angels to help and grant you support.

Deuteronomy 33:12 • 2 Samuel 22:2–4 • Psalm 27:5
Psalm 60:12; 91:1–4 • Proverbs 3:21–26 • Isaiah 43:5

Provision

In the name of Jesus Christ:

All of these blessings will come upon you and overtake you because you obey the voice of the Lord your God: blessings in the city, blessings in the field, many children, ample crops, and large flocks and herds. You will have blessings of fruit and bread, blessings when you come in and when you go out.

The Lord will always provide everything you and your family need if you obey Him and walk in His ways.

Deuteronomy 28:1–14 · Psalm 37:3, 19, 25
Matthew 6:33 · Philippians 4:19

Safety

In the name of Jesus Christ:

I bless you with the confidence that you can lie down in peace and sleep, for though you are alone, the Lord your God will keep you safe. He will let you rest in the meadow grass beside the quiet stream.

You can call on the name of the Lord when you are in danger, and He will keep you safe. If you put your trust in God and not in men, He will put a hedge of protection around you.

When doing right, you will not be afraid but will always rest in peace and safety.

Psalm 23:1–4; 4:8; 119:114; 121 • Proverbs 18:10; 29:25

Spiritual Power

In the name of Jesus Christ:

I bless you with the knowledge that God has given you the ability to overcome the powers of darkness in this world. You have the power to come against unclean spirits and wickedness of every kind.

You will receive this power as a gift from God through the Holy Spirit. It is the same power that enables you to give witness of your faith in Jesus Christ to your family and friends, as well as to all people on any part of the earth. You are greatly blessed by receiving this power.

*Isaiah 59:19 · Matthew 10:1 · Mark 16:17 · Acts 1:8
Ephesians 3:16, 20; 6:10–11*

Strength

------◆◆◆------

In the name of Jesus Christ:

You will be strong and make your boast in the Lord, for He is your Rock. He is your High Tower.

He is the Source of all your energy, and He alone can give power to the faint and increase your strength when you have none. Even in your youth, there may be times when you feel weak, but your strength will be renewed as you wait upon the Lord. You will be empowered to soar like an eagle. You will run and not be weary. You will walk and not collapse along the way.

Call upon Him to give you strength sufficient for every task. May your strength equal your days.

Deuteronomy 33:25 · Psalm 27:1; 46:1
Isaiah 40:29–31 · 2 Corinthians 12:9

Success

In the name of Jesus Christ:

I bless you with a spirit of success. You will not be overcome today or any other day by a spirit of failure, but you will be blessed continually with a spirit of achievement.

You will achieve for God first, then for yourself and others. You will not be prideful because of this, but you will glorify God. It is He who is blessing you with a life filled with successful experiences and happy times.

You will be like a tree planted by a river. Your leaves will never fail, and you will bear fruit as long as you live.

Psalm 1 · Joshua 1:8

Trust

❖❖❖

In the name of Jesus Christ:

I bless you with ability to trust in the Lord with all your heart and not depend upon your own understanding. Such trust will keep you on the right track and bring health to your body, as well.

When you trust in the Lord and do good things for others, you can expect Him to meet all your needs and keep you from harm. You will be a happy person.

When you depart from evil and seek peace, the eyes of the Lord are upon you, and His ears are open to your cry. You can trust Him to hear and answer your prayers and give you the desires of your heart.

Psalm 34:8; 37:3–4 · Proverbs 3:5; 16:20

Wisdom

In the name of Jesus Christ:

I bless you with godly wisdom and discernment. May you always have a reverent fear of the Lord and a respect for His Word, for that is the source of all wisdom.

Keep on growing in spiritual knowledge and insight so that you can always see clearly the difference between right and wrong. This will make you inwardly clean. Wisdom will keep you safe from disaster and make you a happy person.

May you be wise in heart and always be doing those good, kind things that show you are a child of God. This will bring much praise and glory to the Lord.

Psalm 111:10 • Proverbs 2:6–7; 3:13, 21, 23; 16:21
Philippians 1:9–11

Part Three:

The Fruit of Blessing

Your Blessings

Now that you have completed seven weeks of blessing those you love, use the next few pages to write out some blessings of your own. God's Word is full of promises of blessing, and as you read and meditate on your favorite passages from Scripture, His Spirit will guide you in the gift of blessing.

Your Blessings

Your Blessings

A Personal Reward of Blessing

By Elise, to Mary Ruth Swope—"Grama"

When I was twelve years old, my father married my stepmother. That's when I first met Dr. Mary Ruth Swope, my stepmother's mother. At first, I thought of her as a businesswoman who was always on the go, writing books, giving lectures on nutrition, and traveling across the country to make appearances on radio and television talk shows.

Then, when I was eighteen and going through a turbulent time in my life, the woman whom I'd known from a distance as Mary Ruth Swope became a beacon of light in my darkness. She graciously invited me to live with her, and our true knowledge of each other peaked, making us no longer acquaintances but friends.

As we spent time together, I learned that I could trust Mary Ruth with the secrets of my heart. Sharing my innermost feelings and thoughts inevitably brought forth her practical suggestions for weighing problems and her hope-filled words to brighten my dreary thoughts.

Mary Ruth became my confidante, mentor, encourager, friend, and grandmother—even without blood to connect our histories. But most of all, she became a vessel for and a vivid reflection of the love and guidance found in Christ Jesus.

It was only three months into my stay when I asked her if I could call her "Grama," and she warmly accepted me as her only granddaughter.

During the times when I was most distraught, she would draw me close and hold me, asking God to pour out the oil of joy over my mind and heart. Little did I know that these prayers would soon move me from restlessness to peace. Her words stimulated my mind and settled my broken spirit in a way I had never experienced before or believed possible.

When Grama prayed, she usually began in thanksgiving and then moved into a quietness of spirit before the Lord. Our requests mostly centered around an opening of my mind to divine meaning for my life. Each prayer Grama prayed with me was a blessing in and of itself because I always walked away thinking more clearly about myself, my place in this world, and my relationship with God.

By the fifth month of my stay—with Grama praying for me steadily—a feeling of inner peace had settled over my spirit. The bond of trust that had grown between us now inspired me to pray apart from her, and I soon discovered that the act of praying gave me confidence in the fruit of the Spirit found in Christ Jesus.

In addition to Grama's many prayers, which were gilded with thanksgiving and impressionable blessings, her insightful knowledge of Scripture also had a tremendous influence on my life. Near the beginning of my stay, Grama would read passages from the Bible to me. Each passage was applicable to my situation and served as a comfort and a practical guide in the jumble of everyday situations. God's Word helped me find meaning in my personal chaos.

Despite Grama's demanding schedule, I am thankful for the time that she took and still takes to reveal some of the ultimate truths found in the Bible. One of the Scriptures I most remember her relaying to me came from Philippians 4:6. In *The Living Bible*, it reads like this: *"Don't worry about anything; instead, pray about everything; tell God your needs, and don't forget to thank him for his answers."*

Grama also had some of her own words of wisdom. Whenever I would speak of sorrows in my life, she would say to me, "The battle of life is in the mind, Elise!" I now understand this phrase and recall it during times of uncertainty.

Through her love for me, her beaming example before me, her patience with me, her concern for others, her vitality for living, and her contagious sense of humor, a renovation took place inside of me.

Today, Grama's house is my home away from home. Since my first stay, I have been back every summer to visit her. I will be forever grateful to her and thankful to the Lord for using her in my life when I needed tenderness the most. Through her Scripture readings and her example, my attitudes have changed. Through her prayers, my spirit has become whole. I love you, Grama.

May God bless all who read this book, and may children everywhere—of all ages—be changed by the Spirit of Christ that has inspired it.

The Fruit of Blessing

———◆◆◆———

L et me begin with an embarrassing confession. When the Holy Spirit introduced me to the concept of blessing my seven-year-old grandson, I was totally engrossed with the "nuts and bolts" of how to write or speak a blessing. At the time, I did not consider the immense potential for the various types of "fruit" that would accrue.

Much to my surprise, the rewards with Daniel were immediate and were quickly followed by testimonies from other people who were using this book regularly. Let me share a few of the remarkable results that daily and persistent blessings have produced.

Blessed with Good Behavior

The first phone call I received concerning this book came from a woman in Wisconsin.

"I just called to thank you for writing this wonderful little book," she said. "My husband began to bless our three children—ages nine, seven, and two—every day."

She went on to describe the changes in their children's behavior that the daily blessings had produced. The children were:

+ more pleasant,
+ more obedient,
+ more helpful to one another,
+ easier to put to bed at night,
+ more cooperative, and
+ more loving and tenderhearted.

Then, she told me about an incident that had recently occurred. While the children were playing downstairs, the two-year-old child was offended by something that took place. When he began to cry in a screaming voice, his nine-year-old brother went and placed his hand on the toddler's head and blessed him. The crying stopped instantly, and peaceful play resumed. Naturally, both parents were very impressed by this event.

The Power of the Tongue

Soon after the first printing of this book, a Canadian television station invited me to be their guest and talk about it. After two one-hour programs on the subject, the station manager continued to read a blessing on the air every day over the next few days.

Not long afterward, I was surprised to receive a phone call from one of the station's staff members, who said excitedly, "Let me share with you some of the testimonies we have received from our viewers!"

The first testimony came from a woman who had been totally deaf for sixteen years. Although she could not hear, she was able to read the lips of the person talking on the television.

On that day, the announcer was reading the blessing entitled "Listening Ears." The first sentence in that blessing reads, "In the name of Jesus Christ, I command your ears to hear clearly today."

As she read the announcer's lips, both of her ears made a popping noise and were completely healed! Her audiologist later told her that she had the hearing of a teenager and that, as far as he could tell, she had received total healing.

When the words were released, healing came immediately. Unfortunately, prior to this testimony, I had not realized that healing could be received by faith through blessing. My faith in the truth of Proverbs 18:21 was greatly enhanced by this experience. *"Death and life are in the power of the tongue, and those who love it will eat its fruit."*

Blessings by Mail

The second testimony resulting from the television station's daily blessings concerned a young couple with marital problems.

The twenty-five-year-old husband was planning to abandon his twenty-three-year-old wife for a younger woman who worked in his business. After declaring his intention to get a divorce, he picked up his belongings from the house, leaving his wife and two small children to fend for themselves.

The young wife got a copy of this book and used it as a guide to write a blessing to her husband each night before she went to bed. Every morning, on her way to work, she mailed the blessing to him.

At the end of two weeks, the husband phoned to ask if he could return home. The wife was delighted and amazed that her blessings had produced fruit in such a short period of time. I can't help but wonder if she is still reaping the rewards of blessing her loved ones today.

"Thank You for Blessing Me"

The third testimony resulting from the television station's emphasis on blessing came from the mother of a two-year-old daughter. After she had blessed her daughter for the first time, the child said to her, "Thank you, Mommy, for blessing me," and went running to her room to play.

At intervals during the day, the little girl would come to where her mother was working and repeat the expression, "Thank you, Mommy, for blessing me." Regardless of age, testimonies reveal that people love to be blessed!

As I related in the first section of this book, I can still remember the enthusiasm with which my grandson Daniel thanked me the first time I gave him a blessing. He said, "Thank you, Grandmother," with such gusto that you would have thought I had given him a tangible, much desired gift.

Blessings in Reverse

Six months after I had first blessed Daniel during one of our frequent long-distance phone calls, I asked him, "Would you be willing to give me a blessing?"

His answer was a quick and powerful yes—sharper than a two-edged sword, so to speak. "Certainly, Grandmother, just give me a minute." Then, almost immediately, he said, "Grandmother, I bless you with love, with good health, and many more days to live."

Wow! I am still amazed and blessed by the wisdom of my grandson. In fact, I can only add this to his blessing: "Please, Lord, *do it!*"

A Valuable Treasure

The single mom of a nine-year-old boy told me that her son would not let anyone remove this book from his bedside table. He considered it his most valuable treasure and loved to be blessed every night before he went to sleep.

One night, the mother went to a professional meeting. Before leaving home, she told her son, "I won't be home until nine thirty. Just get yourself ready for bed and don't wait up for me."

When she arrived home at ten thirty, she noticed a light shining from her son's bedroom. She entered his room with the intention of scolding him when he said to her, "Momma, I'm sorry I didn't follow your directions. I couldn't go to sleep without you giving me a blessing."

Here is another incident that illustrates how much a parent's blessings mean to even a young child.

When the grandmother of a four-year-old came from out of state to visit, she was thrilled to spend time with her grandson. Soon after her arrival, the youngster went running to his bedroom and came back with his copy of this book. As he handed it to his grandmother, he said, "Grandma, this is the book where they give me hugs after they read it."

The child's mother explained, "He loves to be blessed, and we always follow the daily blessing with lots of affection."

What better gift can a parent give a child?

A Blessed Little Preacher

Another interesting testimony is about a little boy who was just learning to babble in sentences. His parents had spoken a blessing over him every day of his life and even before his birth.

When the toddler's mother took him to his grandfather's office, the secretaries gathered around to see the little boy and coo over him.

The child responded by making gibberish conversation back to them. When they began to laugh, the child became visibly disturbed. He began to use his hands and speak louder, obviously trying to communicate a message he was incapable of speaking in plain English. When they continued to laugh, the little boy shook his fist at them, got red in the face, and spoke even louder.

One of the secretaries went to get the grandfather to watch this episode. The moment he came into the room and saw his grandchild, he said, "My little boy is trying to preach before he can even talk!"

It will be interesting to see if that prophecy comes true. The child is now seven years old, has accepted Christ as his Savior, and is a delightful, obedient little man in the making. His father recently said of him, "Shane declares almost weekly that he is going to preach God's Word to the nations while he is still young. What a gift!"

Trophies and Awards

When a seven-year-old athletic champion was congratulated by his teacher for a trophy he received, he told her, "I know why I won the award."

The teacher responded, "Why is that?"

His answer came back, "Because my father blesses me every day before I go to school."

Children need parental blessings every day, and there is no better way to receive them than from the father of the household first thing in the morning.

Corporate Blessings Work

Blessings don't have to be personal to be effective. Corporate blessings also produce great rewards. In August, just before school resumed for the year, a pastor began to bless the children in his congregation. Every Sunday, he would ask all the children present to come forward for a blessing before they left the main auditorium to attend Sunday school classes.

Later, in May, the local school held its annual award ceremony to recognize the various accomplishments of certain students. Afterward, someone remarked that every award went to a child from this pastor's church—every single one!

It pays to bless one another. It is God's will. A simple act of blessing will result in great accomplishments and aid in producing healthy, happy, godly citizens.

Blessed Students

An elementary school teacher uses this book in her classroom before classes begin.

One morning, she neglected to give the blessing. When one little boy put up his hand, she called on him to speak. "You forgot to bless us this morning," he told her.

"I'm so glad you reminded me," the teacher replied.

"It makes all the difference," she said. "Blessing the children before they begin to work results in better behavior and a more productive learning environment than when they are not blessed."

Three other teachers have related their experiences to me. One taught fifth grade, another seventh, and the other taught eighth grade. These highly qualified teachers had from five to ten years of experience when I met them.

After they began to bless the children, all three teachers noted that the difference between the blessed classes and the non-blessed classes was remarkable. The blessed students were quieter in their spirits, more able to concentrate, more cooperative in helping other students, and more obedient.

Such positive results would certainly be welcome in today's schools, where getting and keeping the attention of students and having them work willingly is a tremendous challenge. Speaking classroom blessings could also be an antidote to any unfavorable home and cultural influences affecting students' behavior.

A Christmas Blessing

Another touching testimony comes from my friends in Idaho. At Christmastime, they told their adult children to prepare for a ceremony after Christmas dinner, during which their grandfather would bless all seventeen children and grandchildren. As planned, they sat together by families in the living room.

When the grandfather started blessing the little ones first, the teenagers giggled, and some even laughed. By the time he came to blessing the parents, however, tears were flowing from almost every eye. The grandmother said it was the most blessed and memorable evening that she and her husband had ever spent with their children and grandchildren.

Tears often accompany emotionally charged times of blessing. When the person giving the blessing speaks under the guidance and inspiration of the Holy Spirit, the words resound as prophecy and deeply affect the recipient's spirit.

Before including this incident in my book, I decided to obtain the family's approval of my description. When I phoned, one of the adult children answered because her parents were out of town. "That's exactly what happened," the daughter told me as I described that Christmas night.

Then, she added, "But the story doesn't end there; it just begins. After that night, many wonderful things began to happen. The healing of deep wounds took place. Miracles of all kinds happened. And best of all, every one of our children has come to the Lord and is serving Him in beautiful ways. We all agree: good things started happening to us after our father gave each of us a blessing that Christmas. Blessing one another has become a family tradition now."

A Blessed Experiment

The parents of an eleven-year-old child described the following incident.

"Our daughter had never achieved mature bladder control and had wet the bed every night of her life," they told me. "After reading your book and using it with success for a few weeks, we agreed on a plan. One night, we put our daughter to bed with a regular blessing and then waited for her to fall asleep. Then, we returned to her bedroom for a blessing experiment."

As their daughter lay sleeping, her parents placed their hands over her body and blessed her kidneys, commanding that they not release urine until the child awoke in the morning. They also blessed every organ in her body and praised God for answering their prayers.

"She never wet her bed again!" they exclaimed.

Blessing Overcomes Cursing

I learned of another incident that may be helpful to many parents.

A thirteen-year-old boy who had grown up in a loving, Christian family was beginning to speak abusively to his mother. Puzzled as to what she should do, the mother decided to bless him with a controlled tongue, which is one of the blessings in the book.

Every day, she said, "I bless your tongue. You will learn early in life to weigh your words before you pour them out of your mouth. Your tongue will always find ways to bring happiness and blessing to others."

"Our daughter had never achieved mature bladder control and had wet the bed every night of her life," they told me. "After reading your book and using it with success for a few weeks, we agreed on a plan. One night, we put our daughter to bed with a regular blessing and then waited for her to fall asleep. Then, we returned to her bedroom for a blessing experiment."

As their daughter lay sleeping, her parents placed their hands over her body and blessed her kidneys, commanding that they not release urine until the child awoke in the morning. They also blessed every organ in her body and praised God for answering their prayers.

"She never wet her bed again!" they exclaimed.

Blessing Overcomes Cursing

I learned of another incident that may be helpful to many parents.

A thirteen-year-old boy who had grown up in a loving, Christian family was beginning to speak abusively to his mother. Puzzled as to what she should do, the mother decided to bless him with a controlled tongue, which is one of the blessings in the book.

Every day, she said, "I bless your tongue. You will learn early in life to weigh your words before you pour them out of your mouth. Your tongue will always find ways to bring happiness and blessing to others."

Corporate Blessings Work

Blessings don't have to be personal to be effective. Corporate blessings also produce great rewards. In August, just before school resumed for the year, a pastor began to bless the children in his congregation. Every Sunday, he would ask all the children present to come forward for a blessing before they left the main auditorium to attend Sunday school classes.

Later, in May, the local school held its annual award ceremony to recognize the various accomplishments of certain students. Afterward, someone remarked that every award went to a child from this pastor's church—every single one!

It pays to bless one another. It is God's will. A simple act of blessing will result in great accomplishments and aid in producing healthy, happy, godly citizens.

Blessed Students

An elementary school teacher uses this book in her classroom before classes begin.

One morning, she neglected to give the blessing. When one little boy put up his hand, she called on him to speak. "You forgot to bless us this morning," he told her.

"I'm so glad you reminded me," the teacher replied.

"It makes all the difference," she said. "Blessing the children before they begin to work results in better behavior and a more productive learning environment than when they are not blessed."

Three other teachers have related their experiences to me. One taught fifth grade, another seventh, and the other taught eighth grade. These highly qualified teachers had from five to ten years of experience when I met them.

After they began to bless the children, all three teachers noted that the difference between the blessed classes and the non-blessed classes was remarkable. The blessed students were quieter in their spirits, more able to concentrate, more cooperative in helping other students, and more obedient.

Such positive results would certainly be welcome in today's schools, where getting and keeping the attention of students and having them work willingly is a tremendous challenge. Speaking classroom blessings could also be an antidote to any unfavorable home and cultural influences affecting students' behavior.

A Christmas Blessing

Another touching testimony comes from my friends in Idaho. At Christmastime, they told their adult children to prepare for a ceremony after Christmas dinner, during which their grandfather would bless all seventeen children and grandchildren. As planned, they sat together by families in the living room.

When the grandfather started blessing the little ones first, the teenagers giggled, and some even laughed. By the time he came to blessing the parents, however, tears were flowing from almost every eye. The grandmother said it was the most blessed and memorable evening that she and her husband had ever spent with their children and grandchildren.

Tears often accompany emotionally charged times of blessing. When the person giving the blessing speaks under the guidance and inspiration of the Holy Spirit, the words resound as prophecy and deeply affect the recipient's spirit.

Before including this incident in my book, I decided to obtain the family's approval of my description. When I phoned, one of the adult children answered because her parents were out of town. "That's exactly what happened," the daughter told me as I described that Christmas night.

Then, she added, "But the story doesn't end there; it just begins. After that night, many wonderful things began to happen. The healing of deep wounds took place. Miracles of all kinds happened. And best of all, every one of our children has come to the Lord and is serving Him in beautiful ways. We all agree: good things started happening to us after our father gave each of us a blessing that Christmas. Blessing one another has become a family tradition now."

A Blessed Experiment

The parents of an eleven-year-old child described the following incident.

The blessing began to take hold in this teenager's life. His mother reported that he no longer spoke to her in a rude or abusive manner. When this mother spoke words of blessing, God Almighty gave her what she spoke.

Blessing Away Fear

Another couple used this book to help their young child overcome a spirit of fear. After moving into their new, larger home, he became afraid to walk down the long, dark hallway to his bedroom at night. He was so fearful that he would neither go to his room nor come out of it without one parent being present.

"This was very irritating and inconvenient for us," the mother told me. "After we read the blessing on the fear of the Lord to him from your book, he never again asked to have someone accompany him to or from his bedroom."

Another family had a different problem, but the cause was also rooted in fear.

When a South African family moved to the United States for a special assignment in the father's profession, their six-year-old child faced many adjustments. For some reason, the boy had an immediate hatred for Sunday school at his new church.

"It was very difficult to get him to go to church or to leave his mother once he was there," the father said. "I began to bless him secretly. Within one week of daily blessing, the little boy changed his mind about Sunday school. In fact, it became his favorite part of the week."

The Blessing Strategy

Blessings work in the lives of adults in the same way that they do in children.

A young woman employed in a marketing firm was having difficulty with a business client who owed her boss $24,000. The client refused to pay the bill because he had not received a business increase commensurate with the cost of the advertising.

The owner of the business, who was a Christian, did not want to take legal action against her customer. "Let's begin to bless this man and his business," the young employee suggested. Her boss thought is was a great idea.

Within two weeks, they received an unexpected check for $20,000 with a note saying that the remaining balance would be coming as soon as possible. In fact, the total bill was paid without any coercion from the advertising agency.

In another incident, a doctor performed surgery for a patient free of charge because of the stressed financial circumstances of the man's family. Later, when it became necessary for the patient to have additional surgery, the patient agreed beforehand to pay the $1,800 fee.

After the surgery, however, the patient had a different attitude and told the doctor that his healing was not worth the price. Instead of becoming angry, the doctor decided to begin blessing the man. Soon, the patient came into his office, gave him $2,000 in cash, and said to call the situation settled.

I'm sure many sour business deals could result in sweet endings by using the blessing strategy!

Blessing Works!

Does blessing children or adults work in developing countries? Or does it work only in prosperous places? This illustration from personal experience answers that question.

Once, while we were visiting Costa Rica, our host pastor told us, "I will pick you up at the hotel on Friday night a few minutes early. I have something I want to show you."

That evening, he drove us to the parking lot behind the Jewish synagogue. He pointed and said, "Look at the kinds of cars in this lot."

I couldn't believe it! Every car was an expensive Mercedes Benz, BMW, or some other luxury vehicle. And this was in a country where most people don't even own a car! The pastor's point? "Jewish fathers bless their children every Friday night at Shabbat," he reminded us.

Apparently, God answers prayers for blessing regardless of where on earth they are spoken.

Bless Your Wife Every Day

One morning, a male friend of mine phoned and told me, "Mary Ruth, I want you to change the title of your book *The Power of Blessing Your Children*."

I replied, "Fine; what do you want me to call it?"

"I don't know what to call it, but I know it works for grown-ups, as well."

"What makes you say that?" I asked.

"My wife was recently going through a time of change in life, and our relationship had deteriorated so badly that we weren't getting along very well," he explained. "One morning, I came to breakfast and made a comment about the orange juice. I don't even remember what I said, but she began to argue with me until it was more than I could take.

"I left the table, went to our bedroom, closed the door, and got on my knees. I began to pray, 'God, this is a case for You. I simply do not know how to handle her.' Immediately, the Holy Spirit said to me, 'Go and get Mary Ruth's book and begin to bless your wife every day before you go to work.'

"I did that, and in less than one month, our relationship had improved so much that we were acting like newlyweds!"

Every husband and wife can rejuvenate their marriage by taking the time to bless each other every morning.

The Power of Spoken Blessings

The concept of the blessing is, regretfully, like that of fasting—a lost theology. Nonetheless, the blessing will always be a tool for humans to use to release themselves and others from insecurities and fears and to unite with one another in intimate relationships. Friendships can be developed, nourished, and permanently cemented through the use of spoken blessings.

The principles of blessing are based on two major Scriptures:

Death and life are in the power of the tongue, and those who love it will eat its fruit. (Proverbs 18:21)

Not returning evil for evil or reviling for reviling, but on the contrary blessing, knowing that you were called to this, that you may inherit a blessing. (1 Peter 3:9)

These two Scriptures provide us with the perfect guidelines for successful family living.

One thing should be clear: we have the ability to influence both our personal lives and the future of our nation through the powerful act of speaking blessings. It is a foundation stone for successful family and community living.

Salvation Prayer

If you do not know Jesus as your Savior and Lord, simply pray the following prayer in faith, and Jesus will come into your heart!

Heavenly Father, I come to You in the name of Jesus. I am a sinner. I ask You to forgive me of my sin. I confess that Jesus is Lord. And I believe in my heart that You raised Him from the dead. Thank You for coming into my heart, for giving me Your Holy Spirit as You have promised, and for being Lord over my life. Amen.

About the Author

D r. Mary Ruth Swope (1919–2018) was a popular lecturer, author, and nutritionist. Born on October 28, 1919, she received a B.S. in home economics from Winthrop College in Rock Hill, South Carolina, an M.S. in foods and nutrition from the University of North Carolina–Greensboro, and a doctorate in administration from Columbia University, New York City.

After seven years of teaching vocational home economics to high school students, she served as a nutritionist with the Ohio Health Department. Dr. Swope later joined the foods and nutrition faculty at Purdue University and then served as head of foods and nutrition at the University of Nevada. As a college administrator, she served as head of the Home Economics Department at Queens College in Charlotte, North Carolina. For eighteen years, Dr. Swope was Dean of the School of Home Economics at Eastern Illinois University in Charleston, Illinois.

After her retirement in December 1980, she begin a new ministry, Nutrition with a Mission. Through lectures and seminars, she encouraged audiences to deny themselves unneeded calories, save the money the calories would have cost, and give it to Great Commission programs and projects.

Dr. Swope made many TV appearances on shows such as *The 700 Club* on the Christian Broadcasting Network and was a seminar speaker at PTL in Charlotte, North Carolina, and Christian Retreat in Bradenton, Florida.